Bryony Blaze wrote from a place of self-discovery, validating emotion, heartache, and love. They wrote sexy poems and devastating poems. Their words bring a light to the lonely human struggle, the queer struggle, and the intangible desire to love and be loved in a broken body.

Bryony Blaze left this world (fuck diabetes) on September 11, 2016. They live on in our hearts, our poems, our dancing bodies, our laughing souls, and the queer space they birthed, "Queer Poetry Takeover." Now too, their words, unedited and combined in this collection, will live on.

AA 2019

# TABLE OF CONTENTS

## Part 1:

7 Flames
8 My love poems are not gooey or cute
10 Breakup Poem to my Mother
12 Scars so deep
14 Nebulous
16 Options
17 I am
18 Together is us
19 14 year old me
23 Myself
24 A lonely place sits in my heart
25 I just want it to flow out of me
26 I'd shrunk myself
28 I am a vintage bottle ready to be uncorked; I have aged well
31 When life throws you curves sometimes you take them
34 Cookies
36 blinders
39 Seeking
40 Shit
41 Ghost pieces of my heart
43 small boxes
47 Portland, Potland, My queer oasis
50 No references
51 The me of me?
53 Looking
54 Foggy Notions
56 Beauty & Beast
57 Precious Moments
59 You taught me everything
62 Living Dante
63 Rising Awry
65 The leaves have fallen, it is clogged with them
67 Falling Forward
69 Over the edge
71 Baited baby's breath
72 Falling into the monster's grasp
76 The light of the darkness

## Part 2:

83 They say it's not violent
86 I Could Have
88 You
91 I want to fuck
94 Possibilities
96 It's too loud
99 The spring rain
100 Get lost
103 Selfish, being good
105 I see you.
106 So,
108 Devilish
109 Sometimes all I think about all day is your pussy.
113 Blow pony
115 I want to unwrap you like the present you are
117 Cunt jumping
125 Cum stains
128 Fruity
130 Hot
134 I don't think you understand how nervous you make me
136 We met after long conversations, took a walk, someplace nice.
137 I want to hear it
141 Cunt Jumping 2 An Ode to the Orgy
149 Wolfs warning
152 Holding onto both sides of the coin
154 Techniques

# Part 1

"This is what I normally write, poetry. It always seems to flow out of me. I get an idea and words spring forth. I also just get one line and work with it. It is mostly an emotional outlet for me, when something happens I just write. I will go back later and revise it, but the first draft is always pretty raw emotion. I love it though and I know most people who read it can feel the emotions I felt or relate to it somehow, which hopefully makes me good at what I love to write." – Bryony Blaze

## *Flames*

As we struggled in our darkness,

In silence and serenity,

We began to fantasize pointed and expansive thoughts,

In our abstract unparalleled world.


We never thought of the pain or destruction it could bring,

We never thought of the ways it could flicker and fade,

Of the ways it could melt us and ourselves.


In our stirring emotions, our beauty, our memories,

We never thought the white hot force would bring our end.


But as it grew brighter,

And as the romance dimmed,

Our light was shown,

And it all made sense.

## *My love poems are not gooey or cute*

Not filled with sweet mush to make you melt

They're messy

Haunted

Dangerous

My poems are full of needles

Blood stains

And hidden gems

Awkwardly placed

If you can see beyond

Where the pretty parts

Are supposed to go

I want the hardened edges

The scrapes

To see them

To touch them

Rub them smooth

Until they fit in the places we need

For you to feel my love sting

The way that only healing love can

I want truth and reality

To help with your bags

Not sweep them under the rug

Bound to show you a better way

This is who I am

Rough around the border

Matching your severity

Together we sync

With our acidity

Eventually the fringes wear

Softer, sweeter in time

This is what a true love poem means

Seeing you in order to see me

Alone we are the only love we need,

On the brink we share it

So come find me

## *Breakup Poem to my Mother*

I took myself from you

Because you never knew how to keep me

You never saw what I needed or

Even what you had by letting me in

When you finally decided you wanted me

It wasn't enough

I took myself from you because you didn't deserve me

Didn't deserve my light, my gifts, my adoration

I tried to show you I was worth it,

Your love, your expression,

Kisses, hugs, words

I tried to be exactly what you kept telling me I wasn't

I am all the things you never could be

I threw away the things you only thought you could see

Because those things were never part of me

You only saw you


I took myself from you

Because I needed safety

Knowing that I was never allowed that from your arms was devastating

Knowing I had to remove me to grow

My heart broke in a million different ways

I still took me from you

Because I knew it was better

That I was better for it

You still never knew

The things you'd placed on me

The things you hadn't recovered from yourself

The lessons you never learned

You've never tried to bridge the rift

So I took me away from you

I just can't break anymore

So I won't

Goodbye

## *Scars so deep*

I didn't see how deep the scars of your love settled

The roots stealed themselves into my soul

Trying to move past

Can't

I reach for the roots,

Tear them up

All I feel are what you've planted

Can't move them out

Still hurts

Years later and the phantasmic barbs of your presence still taint my landscape

A wound only partially healed

Trying to push these roots out of me

Always coming back

The more I try to remove them

I can see the tendrils wrapped around my heart

My muscles

Holding me down

A blackberry bush,

So delicious,

So beautiful

But when you grab

It prinks,

Blood for a sacrifice

Oozing,

Eating your skin,

A lasting moment

Never desired

Avenging youself

Flailing

Pull at the branches

Try to cut the heart of the beast

Never works

Heartache is never resolved

## *Nebulous*

feeling my way across this dark sky

reaching for the closest stars

only to miss

grasping

trying but never holding

hurting

so brilliantly

it can block

e v e r y t h I n g

light unseen

heat not felt

still moving

despite

always despite

locating a refraction

a small smidgeon

something

almost nothing

but I am still seeking

so I lean into it

I roll

finding the small space

where my light shines

burning like the others

combustion

birth of a star

protostellar clouds

collapsing into oblivion

reaching equilibrium

thriving

masses that started

millions of years in the making

generations moved through

all life

bright and blinking

do you see me?

## *Options*

The skies, cloudy but not looming.

They speak of change, of chance, and of possibility.

One way or the other.

Chances come with every wind, they change the course of things.

Nothing is ever certain.

But that is the point of it.

The chances, the possibilities, the limitless skies.

Every dream is spelled out in the wisp of a cloud.

The chance of rain means new outcomes, new challenges.

The expanse of it all screams to take a leap, glide, find what is ahead.

It could be perfect, could be devastating, it could be anything.

But who cares, there is another cloud to life you.

To you elsewhere, just take in the length of one,

breathe one sigh and release yourself to the world.

## *I am*

I am an underestimated mind

stuck in a body for all time.

I am a goddess of my own devices

I am a beauty never to be discovered.

My personality shines yet it is

eclipsed by a shadow.

I am misunderstood in every manner.

I am talent yet unrecognized.

I am but a puppet in a play.

I am a freak of all things.

I am shunned from this cruel world.

I am unacceptable in the eyes of my peers.

I am an unwanted traveler on a weary road.

I am forever alone.

I am forever shut inside myself.

## *Together is us*

Your troubles are mine and mine are yours

Blessed be for all our sores

Your smile melts my heart

My heart melts your mind

You and Yours that I am

My and mine is what you are

My I Love You's and your I Love You's

Are true when they are told.

The light in my eyes shines for

Only you

The flame in your heart burns

Only for me

Together we will end

Together we will begin

And together is where us starts

# 14 year old me

where I return to

every episode of PTSD

14 year old me

when life changed

abruptly

became a survivor

no longer a victim

I always return

14 year old me

victim

driving this adult body

trying to know adult answers

trying so hard to be big in the world

one in which they feel so small

14 year old me


born an old man

already

grumpy, wise, knowing

seeing beyond my years

expansive

living in a child's body

so quickly I grew

stunted

I reversed

became a child

living in a seemingly adult body


from here I learned

life lessons

never grow up

find joy in the little things

a keen eye for bullshit

see meaning in the meaningless

boundaries

room for change

always half of one with a dash of another

perfectly messy

mod podged together

parts of self

they make me whole

help me be

give me rounded edges

bounce

in this oftern too sharp world

except

the 14 year old me sometimes drives the ship

cruising at high speeds

drifting

unsure but too proud

no help needed

I got this


I hide

I shrink into a shell

a fraction

a smaller me than the me I have become

no one should know the wrong

shut it away

shame

silence my own voice

safety

the old man gets more protective

more private

EVERYONE OUT

the small excited child

well she shrinks ever more

almost non existent

there isn't room for joy in fear

14 year old me continues to have control

## *Myself*

I just want to be myself

I've tried and tried, it doesn't work

No one will accept me

Accept me for what I am

For who I am

For who I am going to be

It's impossible to understand

You do not see how much of an outcast

I am

You don't see how I have been treated

How impossible it is for me to fit in

How it will never happen

How I am forever misunderstood

My pain from this is so deep it is

Undetectable

I am but a ghost moving through the shadows

I am a thief never to be caught

I am but a lonely soul

An outcast if you must

Believe me when I say I will never fit in

## *A lonely place sits in my heart*

A lonely place waiting to hear start

A small place that only I know

A small place only I can go

In this place fits a small hand

In this place all are banned

A piece of a missing puzzle

A piece I cannot seem to muzzle

I seek to find the small part that's missing

I seek to find the frog that I've been kissing

In the end I cry

In the end we die

## *I just want it to flow out of me*

creating a river of tears

allowing all the hurt, the heartache to move

move on, move out of me

this pain, I am grateful for hurts so much

I want to feel something else

to feel a touch

a caress

gentle, supportive

sweet, caring

anything

these needles that keep stabbing my eyes

creating a space for themselves

diving in too deep

leaving a divot when they exit

holes to me filled

caked with putty

they will stop leaking

in time

## *I'd shrunk myself*

Like Alice was made to do

To fit through your door

And try to get to you

But you took the key

Locked me out

Traded my bite

And I ate the one without

I was still too big

Too much to swallow

So I bellowed in the doorway

I tried not to wallow

The meaning was there

The desire so evident

But the reciprocation was not

The break became blatant

So I shared my snack

With the others who cared

Surrounded by our tea party

Drinking in the joy

The guilt

The self

Soaking in the heartbreak

And the tears

Steeped in the essence that was

And we became the truth of what could


We became a group to chant

And together we claimed

**Fuck it, we're here**

## *I am a vintage bottle ready to be uncorked; I have aged well.*

I am an onion waiting to be unpeeled, be careful though I will make you cry.

I am that book that takes you so far into it that you have trouble ever coming out of it.

I am that song, with the catchy beat and well-written chorus that gets stuck in your head for days.

I am the piece of jewelry so beautiful you won't wear it for fear of losing it.

I am a piece of art that takes your breath away every time you see it.

I am the tattered ever-present favorite piece of clothing, the closer to your body, the better you feel.

I am that favorite food; the one that the first bite almost sends orgasms through your body.

Yes, I am that good.

I am that first drink on a hot day, so damn refreshing.

I am the beach in between your toes after you have not visited for awhile, ticklish, warm and soothing.

I am the person who makes your whole day once you seem them with big smiles, warm embraces and good conversation.

I am the first sip of your perfectly made coffee in the morning, the one that starts your day off perfectly.

Yes, I am perfect. Maybe perfect for you. But yes, so perfect for me.

I am the blanket you pull out of the dryer on a cold day to get a little warmer.

I am the stuffed animal you cuddle with when sad, the one that has been soaked in your tears but always dries and is always as fluffy as you need them to be.

I am the movie you love to watch over and over again, the one you quote line by line, and the one that comforts you as you see the familiar faces.

I am the flowers you seek when you want something pretty to look at and smell.

I am the familiar face you seek in a crowd when you are unsure, the face that supports and encourages every time you see it.

I am safety; those things you call to when you need it, a hand, a hug, and just a phone call away. I lift you up, I look out for you, and I catch you.

I am that safety net.

I am on the night table beside you, after you have had a dream. You reach out for your glasses; glass of water, whatever is there.

I am there.

I am the toy from childhood that you never threw out, the one that you are happy to see for a second, once again.

I am the song that takes you back to a great year, the year that everything went well and life was happy.

I am the sun after a rainy week, drying you out, giving you a needed break, lifting your spirits again.

I am not failure, it is not allowed within me; I break it, make it impossible and instead I give hope.

I am a comforting visit to your old digs, where you started your own thing.

I am your new digs, the ones you have made your own, that you speak of in light tones, in fragrance, with essence of home.

I am your favorite activity on those rainy days, the one you forget, the one you crawl to when that comfort is needed; you know the one.

I am that cutie you stare at across the room, the one you should take a chance on, the one you should talk to, because it will get you somewhere, wherever it is you wish to go.

I am the start, the lead to a great path, the opportunity of a lifetime, the greatest thing you should never pass up.

I am that thing.

I am that good.

I am there, waiting for you to find me.

## *When life throws you curves sometimes you take them*

When life throws you curves sometimes you take them, running, stride by stride, to the end. But curves are nothing; the hills are what slow you down; the struggle up hill, then going too fast down the other side.

I ran along fine. I was heading towards a good end, finish line in sight, so I thought. The finish line for only the first few mile markers of life anyway. But always at that perfect moment; when things look fine, when the skies clear and life seems good, when everything has fallen into place, ZOOM, a car comes along and steers you off the road. Or that bull on the side charges at you, creating strife, making you cringe and get that "what's gonna happen" nasty look on your face. These looks are what make wrinkles appear on your face later, always reminding you of those times.

This event though, tripped me, brought me down on the pavement hard. Crashing, skinned knees, blood and tears. The sweat became a chill, one I could not get rid of, I hurt, I was bruised and battered, unable to understand why I had fallen, what lead to the falter in my smooth machine, why I was laying on the cold, hard pavement in pain.

My first thoughts were that I had to get up, I had to move, keep going, if not for me, for everyone else too, for my fans, my friends, and my family. The urge to lie there was strong, pain from all over, in trouble and down. I almost wanted to quit, to just stay there, and remain in there in that spot in time. Maybe then nothing else could go wrong. If I was not moving then nothing could change, right? Nothing could hurt me that way. It is surprising how soft and safe the pavement becomes when reality is harsh.

I had to stand, stretch, feel the burn of sore muscles, go on until the end. I needed this. If I did not go on, I felt I would just stop and never start again. I needed to finish. I could rest then. My crutch was the need: the need of others, the need for closure, the need to see what was and what had happened, of what could happen. The disbelief, denial, grieving and crying, all this was part of it, part of everything, part of me, part of life. I had my role. I had my place with everyone. The strong shoulder, I was wanted and had to be, for myself and for everyone. I can deal with the scrapes, cuts and bruises, call them battle wounds, one day scars. Call them blisters and sores, make them bleed and scab; they will heal with time, as will I.

Somehow I managed through the strains, tears, and weak legs; I got up and I started moving again. I was able to pull my feeble body up and wipe away the pain. Slowly at first, stumbling on the suddenly rough pavement, I began. I started to gain ground and things started to even out, my steps became more spaced, easier, more natural. I was beginning to get everything back, my life in order.

I gain speed and my machine becomes oiled again, once broken and shattered, hurt and scarred, feeling old and new, one in the same. Running on renewed fuel and strength, I found somewhere deep within. Overcoming the obstacle that had ruptured my path, I plunged forward, mile after mile, waiting for the next fall, curve or hill.

## *Cookies*

The things around me are crumbling

like cookies left in an oven overnight

burnt and nasty

no taste or texture

they are left to rot

and it isn't just my cookies, but my life

It is everyone, every cookie

40 years means nothing anymore

a promise of marriage forgotten

the idea of commitment

all tossed

chocolate chips or sugar

the cookies are all crumbling

all the money spent to make the perfect cookie

to sculpt the future just right

it was a waste when you forgot they were baking

when you forgot to tend to the small things

they were thrown away when you were thrown away

And here, in this moment

where no amount of mixing

no matter how many therapy sessions

or new ingredients

or even wishing you had changed old ones

it wont change what has already started to crumble

the pieces start to break when touched

they become none of what you had hoped for

the warm, delicious treats you had wished for

or even the life you had planned on

it has been decided for you

you're not going to have these cookies today

maybe you'll start another batch tomorrow

## *blinders*

confused

easily

around you

fogged into feelings

they become me

cannot see

anything else

not even me

only you

us

happy we had

the happy was just a front

an escape

not reality

not the truth

not a thing to be relied on

never a thing to be relied on

choosing to go in

no glasses

blind to the destruction

of me

without the truth

actively pushing past

making that choice

you over me

I accept that

I accept fault with the problem

going with it

jumped in before I looked

knowing I could

knowing the possibilities

broken bone,

but something

hurt self

I still jumped

felt good,

justified

tired of being scared of the world

went with it

now here

hurt

finding I broke me

am I worse off?

or am I better for letting me feel?

long being closed off

is that the pull

wanting to just feel

                                                            Anything

## *Seeking*

feathers to scrub away the dust

putty to fix the scars previously created

an idea in my head

a reality once

can be again

I've seen snippets

I know its out there

seeking

where is the thing that will open me up

expansive and changing

growth and formation

movement beyond this current stagnation

still seeking

wanting to breath the thing that will fill me up

expansion

full to the brim

loving, feeling, releasing

always trusting I will be held

when I fall

lifted when I fly

and saved when it is needed

## *Shit*

Shit happens, everything does

Freaks calm down, people hype up

Lovers quarrel, quarrelers love

Ship mates drown and things go up

Fuckers screw and nerds get fucked

Shit happens, everything does.

## Ghost pieces of my heart

On days like today I can feel them

heavy as the objects that had been planted

I see the outlines of the statue that used to sit there

reminder of our trip to Rome

or the stories of me you used to thumb through

always wanting a little bit more

now neglected

the picture of us in the Eiffel Tower

burns with the background sun


when you changed your mind

you started to take things back

our moments

our memories

empty margins

I forgot existed

moving remnants off the shelves

disrupting our home

dust collected

pooling

leaving unnecessary room

places long filled to the brim

now containing holes


you started to fill these gaps for yourself

reaching in

putting moments there

trinkets of us

snippets

to claim me as yours

it was fine

I was full

we were fine

you started to disappear

taking with you

e v e r y t h i n g


The ghosts of the valued possessions you took away when you left

They no longer exist here but sometimes I can still feel them,

loaded as the day you placed them

on that shelf space in my heart

## *small boxes*

we can call it Pandora's

full of things locked away

took it off the shelf to hide away

safe keeping

too many feelings

too much everything

a box no one fits

used to pack away

all the pieces that just don't fit

chopping Pandora

little bits

things that feel acceptable

hiding the rest

round limbs

stored in square boxes

awkwardly subjected

squished

locked away

only to be seen when its finally safe

but it isn't ever safe

we're never safe

it became something else

something too protected

too much to let go

Pandora was a sham

but I took it off the shelf

to help you

to not hide

I am tired of hiding

we thought

those keys held the answers

secured the wounds

shuffled

they were lost

but you found them

we opened it up

let it out

for you to see

for all to see

sweeping off the dust

no longer pushing the contents down

away

allowed it

cautiously flinging

out came memories

feelings unadultered

unaltered

open

you saw what was there

only to lock it up again

shove it away


its too late

I no longer care

Pandora's whole

out and growing

I am tired

I am here

I demand you see me

demand that which I deserve

demand my freedom

fuck the boxes

the hiding

the hurt

open

full

making it all happen

trusting

me, the magic

life

trusting

## *Portland, Potland, My queer oasis*

I wish to get SO fucking high all I can feel is you touching my skin

Carressing me in the way you do

Firm but soft, tender yet gritty, stinging and coy

The juxtapose of all things wonderful

I want to get so damn stoned that my brain is surrounded ONLY by thoughts of you touching me

Feeling you next to me an wanting to wrap myself in you

Feel you melting into me

Your amazing nature

How you nurture me

How you know me

Your amazing nature

How you know me,

Every inch of me

You teach me, on a daily basis

More about me and so much more about you

And how I love to let you

I can feel you, everywhere

Your kiss, your lips, your hands and your body

I see these things in everything, everyday

In the rain and the way it fondles my skin

In the food, how it reaches me

coaxes me and entices me

On the roses and in their smell,

so beautiful but they have a bite too

I want to smoke until I can't think and all I can do is feel

I can't concentrate enough to even try to touch your skin

I want to, don't get me wrong, I SO want to

But it only plays through my brain, because,

Well

I am too fucking high

I can't move, I can't speak and I choose not to

I am in this moment

Surrounded by everything and nothing

I hunger to feel every sensation in its entirety

Let things go as they may

I want you to write you story on my skin

Trust me with your secrets

And let me be the keeper of your desires

Let your instincts guide you

I want nothing else to exist around me but you

Doing what feels good for you, but oh so good to me too

Then again, right now, EVERYTHING feels good

However,

I don't aspire to be so high that I am falling asleep

But I need to be so close that I could if you were to stop for too long

I want to be so damn high I am basically useless

I crave to be your play toy

Something you covet and cherish

Something you use until you are done

Until I am so exhausted, so worn I have no choice but to sleep

I yearn to be so damn high that the world outside of this

Outside of now

It doesn't exist

## *No references*

For those that don't know that philosophers are poets

I don't give you any answers

I never tell you a lie

I just make you look deeper

I ask you to seek more

I show you all the differences and then I point out all the similarities

The more I see, the more I look

The more you answer, the more I ask

I am never done

Even in the conversation, in the "solution," we are never done

There are more why's, how's, and always a new question after that

I can't give you answers because mine are different than yours

I am still seeking; I never give you full answers

Because I still haven't found one that fits for me

The need for it grows, but the more I grasp, the less I know

The more I get, the less I find compatible

Poets will always be the compass

But you only go where you need

And never where you thought

## *The me of me?*

Were you just a mirror?

So connected to me at all points that I bled into you?

Are you just a reflection of what is inside of me?

Even at this point so connected it is unseen.

I can't recognize me in you.

I can't even recognize the you that was.

But I am not the same, I've changed.

I marvel at my ignorance.

I see what is, I can choose to ignore it, but I can never unsee it.

Is that what you are?

A pocket of the me I used to be.

Stuck in a time lapse that never started again.

Are you susceptible to my imprints?

I am literally the yin to your yang.

Without one the other never moves.

The stasis becomes circular, never amounting to anything more than beyond today.

Are you just the me that I could be?

The me that wished for normality.

The version that erupts when the world gives me everything I asked for?

Are you what I would be if I wasn't through with my lessons, with my life?

Are you the me that can't be because I became me?

## *Looking*

In this world full of beauty what do we perceive as art

every rock, every nail, every crack or do we hold it higher

do we save the world for something that speaks unto us

can art be that scratch on a paper or litter on the street

can it be everything which we see

then does everything deserve praise

and will we admire it all

will we give all things the name

name of beauty, of ideas, of dreams

everything does not need such a name there is a special spark in all of the world

even then worst of scenes

we can judge, recognize, and appreciate but that does not mean it is art

does not mean it needs, deserves or is willing to be praised

does not mean it can be sold for thousands

it just means every day its beautiful

look for this

## *Foggy Notions*

pushing my hands in the air,

trying to wave away this gloom

unable to see the path before me

each inch dangerous

these feelings well up

surrounding

hard to pull out

hard to wade through

hard to get over

the fog isn't lifting

it is only getting worse

more dense

I am yearning for an escape

this haze has me wrapped up in its confusion

no clarity

the light house I had relied upon to steer my ship

has been darkened to the truth

I am still seeking

despite the obscurity

for in the movement

the murkiness never seems to end

and we require transparency

## Beauty & Beast

You are my beauty

I am the beast

You are kind, gentle, beautiful, and passionate

All I am not

I am cruel, sorrowful, uncaring

All that you never want to be

Teach me your ways

Let me live in the light of your sunshine

I wish for you to be my master

I am your student always

Make me yours

I am yours

Till the end... of time

I am cruel and you are gentle

Uncaring and selfish in my ways

Will you teach me? forever?

What I need

What I need to change

I'll give you all that I can

I'll give you all that I can

All that I can

## *Precious Moments*

When you tell me I'm perfect

sometimes I believe you

and when you say I am beautiful

then, that's when I see it

And the times you explain how you love me

I am so sure, I know it


In these moments is when I feel, feel everything


When you look in my eyes, I am peace

and when you take my hand, I am whole

When you hold me close, I shine

and when you smile just for me, I am the world


In these moments is when I am perfection, for you, and now for me


Why after long talks I become vibrant

and a night in your arms revives me

how a fight can bring us closer

and our insatiable appetite for fun can brighten any day

In these moments is when I am amazed by you, how I found you

When you come to me after a long day

and when you kiss my lips

how we fly to each other, and how we flew

and how you take care of me and I, you

In these moments is when I see how empty life used to be

All of these moments, all of this

all of you and all of me

and everyday

again and again, over and over

In this moment is when I fall again, everyday deeper and more in love with you

## *You taught me everything*

You taught me everything, remember.

You showed me love, you showed me hate.

You showed me abuse and you showed me lies.

You showed me hope and you showed me defeat.

And You showed me power, a place I never want to be

You taught me everything, remember.

You taught me give and you taught me to receive

You taught me the joy of pain, it brought me to my knees.

You taught me of distrust and of frustration.

And you taught me of hurt, the strength of a hand.

You taught me everything, remember.

I learned of parents and I learned of children

I learned when you shut up and I learned how to stay beat down.

I learned the meaning of destruction and devastation.

And I learned how to cope and rebuild.

You taught me everything, remember.

I exemplified the horror I knew.

I exemplified the hate I saw.

I exemplified the depression I felt.

And I exemplified the fear you gave.

You taught me everything, remember.

I began to live when I felt left.

I began to understand, I began to see.

I began to feel and I began to form.

And I began to realize all of your wrong.

You taught me everything, remember.

I became strong, I became good.

I became powerful, but now on my own.

I became a woman, I became happy.

And I became what you never thought I could.

You taught me everything, remember.

I am amazing; I am beautiful.

I am living and I will continue.

I am a person and I will be happy.

And I am still realizing that

**YOU DID NOT TEACH ME SHIT.**

## *Living Dante*

Frustrated with life, frustrated with things.

Frustrated with crap, and all of the rings.

Going through hell, all of the scenes.

Going through life, all of its means.

Living a lie, living a dream.

Going in and out of Dante's big themes.

On top of the edge.

Flowing over the gauge.

Living in the motion, living in still.

Having a blast, feeling the chill.

Hell's not the place I want to be.

But it seems to be the place that chose me.

## *Rising Awry*

Why do I suffer?

Why should I change?

Everything changes, why should I

in this dim lit room

and my dim mind

with my closed heart?

Why do I experience, with such closed

eyes, ears, mouths and minds

my life, my love, lost

to the unkind, to the hurt?

How is this possible?

Why do I feel?

What is behind

confusion, exhaustion, frustration?

How can this be?

What brings joy, what brings sorrow?

Why do I cry when I hold nothing?

nothing inside, nothing to hide

Right?

Have I gone left, awry

Where am I? What is this?

Consequences I know none

I know not of

nothing

When, how: life

Saying is not believing.

What is belief?

An existence, a state, a horizon

Look at how the sun sets and rises

Am I rising?

Are you looking at me?

Watching the way I watch you?

## *The leaves have fallen, it is clogged with them*

The leaves have fallen, it is clogged with them. The bridge is getting "shorter" or so it seems.

It really is not but the water is getting higher as the mountains melt and they run off the hills

Into the small creeks that stretch upon each piece of property. This is always a dangerous time of year,

All the water cascading down, washing with them all the fall leaves, creating massive build ups for the

Flow to contend with, all around me the branches poke out, barer than they were just a week ago.

You can see the fallen tree, it has been rotting for years, but at the moment it has a light dust of snow

That fell last night. Yes, this late in the year it still occasionally snows. The water gurgles around me, as i

Watch a deer amble across the meadow. I watch it slowly feel the way to the patches of grass that sill

grows this late in the year (or early depending on how you look at it). The horses are corralled for now.

So this deer is lucky to have a good eating all to himself. As I sit in the serenity that washes over me

With nature I hear the car start to approach on the highway. Will they speed part or are they coming?

Home? Has it been that long yet? When the car turns into the drive way the deer looks up, watches it

Carefully, then bounces off to safety.

I can remember the flood of "96 . how the bridge was torn down. We were not allowed to go near the

Water for fear of flash flood. It was that high that year. It was a culmination of a long early winter and

a freak rain storm that went on for days. We stayed in a lot. Watched movies and just watched on the

tv what was happening. When the weather broke we went down to the meadow to survey the damage.

The horses had been put away safely away from the raising water. We saw a lot of wood. A lot of what

we had swum in over the summer had been washed away. The trees seemed so bare and so distraught

looking. Like they had just been through the wringer, which we knew they had. One of the larger,

branched threes lost its battle; it was in a clump over the creek. Maybe a makeshift bridge the animals

would use to escape something harrowing. We opted not to cut it up. It would be fun to sit on come

summer again. The creek even ravaged was still a safe place for us to play in virtual freedom of the adults.

## *Falling Foward*

Even as you lie here beside me I am lost.

What do I feel, what runs through me?

Is there ice in my veins.

Am I denying the truth.

Why am I crying while you are here.

Why do thoughts of the past plague me.

Am I really falling?

Or do I just want to.

Do you know me, the real me?

Would you still love me then?

Would you still say all the things you've said?

Would you mean them.

The hurt wells, the pain resurfaces.

The past is here.

Am I too scared to move on?

Or is it even real.

Lonely for so long, am I getting what I want.

Or am I pretending.

But I still sit here in the dark.

Watching you sleep.

Watching you be.

Wanting to hold you to be held by you.

Feeling nothing because I push it away.

Missing what's not there and wanting what you say to be true.

Long term, are those your plans.

What are mine

Am I happy, is it true.

What happens next.

I am confused.

## Over the edge

The fear

It over powers me

Surrounds me, overwhelms me

But it is not what you think

It can't hurt me

It can't paralyze me

It can't, I won't let it

To control, to be alive, to be.

I shrink, shrunk, shrank

But I survive

I become

Chrysalis, a butterfly of beauty

Wholesome and wonderful

Approaching the waterfall

Approaching the edge

Do I dare jump, is this how it is

Overcome the fear overcome the pain

Though words have stabbed,

Words have hurt,

Words have made me cry.

Do I dare, do I try, am I

Surrounded by beauty and surrounded by joy

The silence of water, yet the thunder of rocks

Is everything this collision of beauty and pain

Will life always be like

Like this

Flowing, stopping, jagged, smooth, burning and soothing

I lean forward just a little

It's enough, I am over

## *Baited baby's breath*

The cries of a baby and those of the heartbroken are not any different.

Both are seeking,

Gasping for air,

Wanting for nourishment

The love does not exist

The substance they desire

                                      Cannot       be       resolved.

Cries of pain,

Cries of hunger

Cries of solace.

When dealing with a break up

We revert to a simpler stage,

A part of life no one understands.

They can't and they don't even try,

We cannot seem to bath ourselves,

Feed ourselves

Or move beyond a single position,

Curled up,

Rocking,

Wailing.

This is where things used to be,

Things we are no longer allowed.

Suddenly it's all changed

Now with a lack of knowledge,

 A lack of understanding;

It piles against us

 And we struggle.

    Reaching toward whatever we see,

Clinging,

Things that may be able to suffice

But they never do

And like babies we are left to whimper

Wanting

Not finding

Not knowing why

Why we can't have

        Until we get distracted

        A shiny toy,

        Delicious snack,

        A bright new smile,

But only for a second

The hope of something,

A glimpse of future sun,

A breakthrough,

                Until the ache starts again.

## *Falling into the monster's grasp*

It's always easy

Always the seduction

Purred words in my ear

Caressed in a way

It feels safe

Full

Promises

Hope

Extra attention

Extra everything

All empty

The monster you hid behind gifts

And praise

And words

All the extras for extras sake

So I would feel whole

Taken care of

Superficially lifted

It stops,

You come out of hiding

It's hard to see

Behind the monster's you surround yourself with

They won't see it

They're monsters too

Maybe I knew in my bones

Maybe I had an inkling

Told myself not to

Said no

But truthfully let you

Walk right through the door

Get into my being

Into my head

My life

Wrapped myself into you

Because for some reason

I like monsters

## *The light of the darkness*

The darkness is all around us, but there is a light.

The light is so painful but the darkness is bright.

We drift toward the darkness out futures unfold.

We drift toward the light our feelings untold.

The light consumes us to our dismay.

The pain we feel grows more each day.

We get split apart by the shadows of the light.

Yet still by our souls we are wounds tight.

And so far apart, the light holds the dark.

Across the world you maybe.

But when I close my eyes, it's you that I see.

We are thrown together by destiny by fate.

Our lives are not separate by the hour of late.

Our minds are like one in the bottle marked fate.

Yet they will not leave this wretched state.

Our minds are made up now, the reasons are clear.

Our paths are staked out, that's why I hold you so dear.

This future we hold, its yours and its mind.

And somewhere along the path they intertwine.

Our souls are so foggy, its gripping our sphere.

Its kind of trippy how we can think so clear.

But thinking's not the answer, both you and I know it's true.

Yet the world we live in, we both know is cruel.

The pain we deal with cannot turn to fear.

We leave this world shedding one single tear.

# PART 2

"I am nervous, unsure, shy to a point. I believe what people tell me now. I see it. But I don't understand why I am denied what I seek. A simple audience with you. A simple hello, a smile (if I don't look away out of shyness), or a drink, to loosen me up so I can relax. I often think of a simple line (how much does a polar bear weigh?? Enough to break the ice) or a compliment, nice hat, cute shirt, cool glasses, awesome hair. I often, when in a presence, or even not, guess at who you are. Wanting to know. Always imagining, putting things I see into it. Sometimes I get a reality check.. your voice is not what I had vaguely imagined it sounded like. And also, curious what is under the clothes, I have preferences yes, but maybe for you maybe I can go another route. I have had dreams dappling of what may be, come or well, whatever. Mostly G-rated and cutesy. But even those I wake up and have to go with the urge. I feel hot, I feel happy and when the dream ends, well I want more." – Bryony Blaze

The following poems are a collection of Bryony's "sexy" poems. They read many at Portland's "Dirty Queer" and at "Queer Poetry Takeover." They are cutesy and sometimes explicit.

## *They say it's not violent*

They say that it's pleasant

To me it feels like ripping.

Peeling back my skin

Exposing my insides

Organs to the sun

Things that were never supposed to see the light

But you asked

I crumbled

Broke under the weight of your love

Trusted your hands

Your heart

You tried to mend me with surgery

Undid each of the stitches

The ones I had

Skillfully placed to make me whole

My Frankenstein remake

You knew the scars that were covered in makeup

Saw the face that was just a mask

The costume I wore that was becoming unglued

Skin underneath

Soft and supple

Had been wrapped carefully in cloth

Bandages,

Fresh and new like a baby's breath

Tender

You moved forward

Continue to explore

Eventually you tore right in

Searching for the pieces to put back into place,

Like you were playing operation

I cried in pain

Exploded with light

Ripped at my own skin.

Searing my insides

Inspect myself thoroughly

A proper autopsy.

Picking the pieces off my bare bones

Like a vulture

Until I knew me

Inside and out

Writhing with every new feeling

Excited to move forward

Sutured from this round

Raw, expressed,

Ready to heal again

I am seeing me finally

So I turn right back around

Handing it over and repeating

To anyone who will listen


Here is my scalpel

Are you ready to begin?

## I Could Have

I could have done a million things.

I could have danced with you.

I could have gone home with you,

Could have gone home with her,

Could have gone home with him,

Could have fucked you,

could have fucked her, him both of them.

I could have, danced a little pulled you close,

slide my hands over you feel your body, feel you.

I could have kept doing that till you couldn't resist anymore.

Till you kiss me.

I could have even just made out with you.

Waited till that moment when I get close enough,

so close that you go that extra inch. And you touch me.

But I will touch you too,

make you wet,

make you want me so bad you beg me to come home,

I could have asked her up for a drink,

or a smoke

or a fuck.

I could have.

I want to say something, something witty, not drunken nor sounding stupid.

But god fucking knows I didn't'.

I want to, or my god I want to so bad,

I want the knowledge that I can and I will.

I want to see you dripping in sweat,

I will lick it off, taste the sweet saltiness of it.

Knowing you have worked every inch of me and that I have you.

Knowing that when we wake in the morning it will happen again.

Every inch of me aching and telling me now,

but I want so much, and I want it so bad I cannot deny it.

I want hands all over me,

in me and around me,

I want lips everywhere.

Sucking,

Biting

and kissing.

I want parting and sliding and wetness,

I want everything I can take and everything you have to give.

I take nothing.

I am the girl in the background, unnoticed, but content with the view.

The girl who knows everything,

meets everyone, but is not seen, not remembered.

I am here,

See me,

Kiss me,

Fuck me.                                          I am waiting.

## *You*

Yes You..

You should see me naked.

Yes you should definitely see me naked.

Curves in all the proper places,

An ass that doesn't quit

Tits that scream grab me, feel me, pull me, lick me.

Just **touch** me.

Imagine me naked just in my docs...

Yes those are **MY** fuck me shoes..

All my tats, all my piercings.. all exposed

In my Doc Martins

Do you see it?

Standing scantily lit, biting my lip..

Waiting for you to come up behind me.

Waiting for you.

Push up behind me,

Against the wall.

I told you, you should definitely see me naked.

In clothes I'm all awkward, always pulling

Pushing something over an imagined roll,

(maybe not so imagined)

Sucking something in,

Being self conscious

But when I see me naked..

**Wow**

I feel like I should walk around like that.

No clothes, not hiding, being me.

I look good, why should I cover up?

The ripe juicy curves of my ass, my hips, my stomach

The perky potency of my breasts

The steady thickness of my hips.

And the readiness of my hands.

That dirty mischievous troublesome glint in my eye.

You've seen it.

I can get you in that good kind of trouble, the kind you giggle at days later.

I know I do.


I don't want to commit.

I did, recently.

And it did not work

I was finding a place for me, but it didn't fit.

I didn't fit.

And now it's MY time.

And I don't want to commit.

I want to have fun.

I want to play.

I want to live each day to every full advantage it brings.

I want to discover new things, new bodies, new loves.

I want to fall in love so many times, everyday I cant keep track of who it was or why.

I want to feel a biting presence today,

And tomorrow a low key chill one.

I want adventure.

I want lazy days.

I want love, to make love, to fuck with love.

But I want the anger too.

I want the passion, the pierce drive and competition.

You think you can make me come?

## *I want to fuck*

I want to cuddle

I want to hold hands

I want to kiss

To make out

To fondle

To be fondled

I want to know you want me

I want you to touch me intimately

On more than one occasion

I want to lean into you

I want you to touch my stomach

My side lightly,

In a very intimate gesture

But discreetly too.

 Want when I put my arms around you and pull away your hand lingers on mine for just a bit too long.

I want that simple kiss to be intoxicating and you linger, reach for another.

I want you to fall in love repeatedly

Everyday I bring something new and you like it.

I want to find new things you love on a daily basis.

In bed, out of bed.

I am an avid learner and right now I insist on studying you.

Watching you, feeling you, enjoying you.

I will take your lead.

I go with your flow.

I'm not imagining the things you could do to me,

Nor am I picturing what I want to do to you.

My heart beats a little faster

My wet cunt pulls me nearer

My anxiety swells

I get goofy eyed,

Linger longer than I feel comfortable,

Walking as close to you as I can get

Hoping to show you I want you.

Hoping you'll have me.

I hate that I can't say anything

I get so overwhelmed

And so frustrated

And so tired of the thoughts of you in my head

The thoughts of hoping to get you into my bed, my life

I hate that I can't say anything.

I am not thinking dirty things,

Dirty words or what music I want playing while we fuck.

I am not aggressive or very confident

But you are… take me, please, I beg.

Try me on for size

I bet I fit

Just right

But seeing you twice a year, it really fucks with me.

So go away, I really fucking hate this

I wouldn't do any of this

I don't want it

I just wanted to let you know

For everything you do, I really do hate you.

I think I need a drink

I don't want you

Can't stand you

I won't do it

I think I might be lying

## *Possibilities*

All the endless, amount less, insurmountable possibilities

All the hopes

All the dreams

All of the adventures to come

All of the things to be had

Possibilities

Do you see the road trips that are in my head

The fun to be had

The beach, our toes in the sand, the burn you got

How I slathered you in sunscreen but it did not work (we laughed too much)

Running out of the hotel naked at midnight to the cold cold water

Then creeping back into the hotel room to warm up by the fireplace

Covered in goosebumps, freezing water and sea scum but giggling for hours

Do you see the possibilities?

Friday afternoon, nothing to do but cuddle and watch a scary movie

The gory not so scary but more gross kind, the ones that even I sometimes turn away from

And as you need to cover your face you lean into me

I grab your chin and pull up for a kiss until it is over

We may not catch the end of this one.

Do you see the possibilities?

The lunch date I want

We have hours to kill, we have a lunch date

We wander, wrapped in each other's company.

Not wanting to make a decision because then we much sit down and eat

Which means we won't, we won't be so close

Wont accidentally (on purpose) touch hands or arms or anything else.

Do you see the possibilities

Going to pick out fish I have already named.

A boy and a girl

I have picked out the boy's name

You get to name her

I will take care of them, they are ours!

We grab the bowl, the rocks, the food.

Do you see the possibilities?

Breakfast in bed (because I couldn't sleep and watching you sleep is the best in the world right now)

A simple gift because it reminded me of you

A flower because I thought of you

A night out because you deserve it

Your favorite drink (coffee, tea or otherwise) brought to you at random.

Do you see the possibilities?

I see how I can fill your world.

Will you let me?

## *It's too loud*

Too loud to talk

Anything but what we are already doing

The dancing

And the flirting

With our body language only

And smiles, very cute coy smiles

And bashful looks away.

I lean in, try to get closer

You resist, but not for long

You try to shy away but my sway baits you

And you meet me halfway

Which Is all I need.

I have my in.

And I take full advantage.

Sink into you a little more.

Touch you just a little bit.

Yes, it is too loud to talk.

To loud to do anything but what we are already doing.

Moving in time to each other

In succession with the music

Gyrating, palpating, inducing a hunger

Thus, when we kiss,

With greedy yearning,

Exploring and fumbling

As I slowly draw my lips to your neck

And you moan

I can ONLY feel it.

I can feel your vocal cords pulse with the noise

The throaty sound escaping you.

And though I can't actually hear it, I imagine it.

And you move,

You slide in,

As close as you dare to get.

But I crave your presence I want it firmly against mine

You move forward to show me you require this too.

I retort with my hands, with my lips and in time with my hips

Yes, it is too loud to talk to whisper secrets or to share our desires

You lean in to touch me,

Slip over my skin,

Bite at my neck.

Now I am reacting with **MY** vocal cords.

They are vibrating to the wetness that surrounds my sex now

They are trembling with the thought of you.

The hotness of your body.

Watching you as you writhe in pleasure.

Seeing you twist in anticipation and voracity.

My mind is reeling with multiple thoughts and images.

A plethora of interlaced ideas.

A mirriad of tender and lewd.

I want to fuck

I want to cuddle

I want to nibble at you

I want to hold your hand

I want to kiss, to make out ferociously.

I want to press you against that wall and let the animal living inside of me

It is definitely too loud to talk.

## *The spring rain*

Only a little cold

I walk home in it

But walking home, leads

To stripping down in it

Getting down to the least I

Can be in public

Letting it hit me

Making me a little cold

Making my nipples hard

Making me giggle, **I LOVE IT**

Touching me as I walk

It makes me hot; The cold rain

I run my hands through my hair,

Over my shoulders

Down my cleavage

It makes me moist too,

All of It literally

I need a deck, or a roof

Somewhere I can stand

Naked in the beauty the rain holds

Come with me?

## *Get lost*

Lost in my eyes, lost in my stare,

Partly due to the intoxicating color of my eyes and because you just like the adoration you see when I look

At you.

Lost in my hips, you have seen them move, you know they are capable of more than they seem.

Lost in this conversation, lost in a discussion, you know how passionate I can get about, well anything and

Everything. I learn and learning is conversation, is new things, is old things, is known things and now

Unknown things.

Lost in my bed, two reasons, you wish to lay down and my bed is comfy, lots of pillows, blankets and it is

Huge (why does a small statured person like me have a big bed, cause I like the room) and two because you

Wish I would come and lay down with you, and yes eventually I make my way over, what comes next, who

Knows.

Lost in whatever it is we are doing, anything, simple, or stupid, just reading, or writing. Anything get lost in it because it is

With me that you are doing it. And you like it.

Get lost.

So lost time flies and you realize you were supposed to be somewhere hours ago. Opps, but the time was

Never waisted. And you will pay the consequences because you felt those hours were better spent.

Get lost in dancing, because it brings you closer to me and you know I like it. But you do need to reach and

Take me by the hand and bring me closer or I will do my own thing as I just love to dance.

Get lost in singing, it is cathartic, cute and helps me know your taste in music.

Get lost in drinking, but not too lost (I don't like an alcoholic) but enough so that you have courage to kiss

Me, as you know I don't, but you know how I lean into you, into our talks, that I want to.

Get lost in touching, the little ones, the big ones, I feel and see and take in every time you do. It makes me

Swoon, makes me get lost and giddy.

And I try to return the favor but am unsure if you are paying attention to that small furtive hand on your

Shoulder for a second or two. But I really hope you do.

Get lost in my hug, don't let get. It is my super power. I am good at it and though I get nervous it has been

Too long I still want to touch you. So pull me back in.

Get lost in the movie, only because you are sitting next to me and all you can think of is that our

Arms/hands/whatever accidentally touched, and as you hear how I breath you know I am lost in that same

line of thought. Who really needs to pay attention to the move anyway?

Get lost in the nerves, but don't let them consume you or nothing gets done.

Get lost.

Lose your self in the flirting, you know I am doing it, so put on the charm.

Lose yourself in the newness, but not too much that you only want that and never appreciate the comfort

We have built together.

Lose your self in us, in building, in learning and growing. Just lose yourself.

Are you up for getting lost? Because I know I am.

## *Selfish, being good*

I am trying, trying to be good, but what the hell is good??

I know being good does not feel good. I want to feel good.

I want to be held, kissed, touched. I want to feel hands on me, to feel lips on me, to be poked and suckled

And to be appreciated.

To know that someone sees, feels and can appreciate my curves. Probably in a way and much better than

Even I can.

I want to be fucked, in the right way, not in the awkward and self-conscious way but in the way, it takes to

Make me cum.

I want my legs to quiver in anticipation. I want to be surprised at how I feel.

I want to be so wet I have to change my underwear three times throughout the day because all I can think of

Is when you come over tonight.

I want to feel legs around me.

I want hands to slide **EVERYWHERE.**

I want kisses sweet kisses, rough kisses, all kisses.

I want lips and teeth in just that right, dirty combination that both is scintillating and delectable.

The right touch, firm and rough yet uncanning soft and supple.

I want to cum, cum so many times the waves ride into each other.

I want to cum at your single touch because I have wanted you, wanted this so bad and so much and at last it

Has been released.

I know I want it all, I also know I can't have it all but I will take some of it. But I am trying to be good.

A small touch no one deems anything leaves my skin burning, aching and still wanting.

Those loose hips on the dance floor and the beat make it hard, the curve of your breast in the loose yet kind

Of tight shirt and the way, you look in that sly hat,

I look away because, well I am trying to be good. But you make it SO hard!

Oh you should see the movie that plays across my mind.. any number of scenarios I have heard of happening to others

Or could happen to me.

You following me (and yes unbeknownst to me) to the bathroom, one of the skeezy queer ones the straight bar bathrooms always lock. Ones that the door never quite shuts right, as I am coming out of the stall you push me back in. or we could do the I am coming out and you happen to be walking in and you push me against the wall before you head into the stall.

Or that look, the one you give the girl who is walking out, that maybe you did not notice before, but in the full bathroom light you see now… how the fuck did you miss her??

All of this I see, I want, I hear. But I am being a good girl, no false fucking, no slippery wet hands inside,

None of all that i have imagined and yes, I imagined a lot.

Seems to be a lot of me at home, on my own, keeping myself well… occupied…

## *I see you.*

I see you as you want to be seen.

Amazing, fuckable but mostly unattainable.

But I have seen you, otherwise unavoidable, reachable and forever keen. I have seen.

Those who don't reach you

Never try

Those who do not appreciate or see you

Only fuck

But I see you. As that venerable wants to be seen by someone.

Wanting to be fucked to be held, to be loved

But…

You can't be that. Not right now, not until you are sure, not until you see.

Not until you see, me.

See who I am.

Who I am to you, who I am on the inside, who I am hiding.

Maybe one day you will see me, maybe as I see you.

Fulfilled, self-loving and whole, but as one.

As a person and willing to be giving, accepting and to become an equal part of a whole.

But maybe I see you as everyone else sees me.

## *So,*

You.

Yes you.

You HAVE seen me naked.

Do you agree?

I wander around, often without clothes, well most of them anyway.

I get caught up in what I look like, what you see

If you notice that my gut has swelled, or the mark on my leg.

I wonder if you see where I have scuffed myself, or if you can point out the mark that you have left.

But then you come up to me, kiss me and caress my back.

I have forgotten about all the things I was so worried about.

I forget about the thoughts of chubby, unattractive me.

I am instead now concentrated on the smoothness of your hands touching me.

Skin to skin

How warm and gentle your lips are and how extravagant it feels when you nip my neck just a bit.

I am no longer concerned, as you escort me to the bedroom, at how my ass looks as it bounces or if my

Thighs are too big.

And when you throw me down onto the bed, I am not worried if I look seductive or if I just look goofy.

As you maneuver me in the positions you like

And you slowly cuff me to the bed so I stop moving, I begin to notice the determination in your eyes.

The look of hunger completely converting your face.

It surrounds me and I can only think of how good you will feel inside of me.

I can only wait now until that perfect moment when you push up into me.

That complex space of climax with relief.

Always because I have been waiting for this point since we started this dance.

That exquisite instance in which nothing but you and I exist (and even then, sometimes not even you.)

That silent state of ecstasy

So in touch with my body, with the energy that is being released at the singular juxtapose.

The debilitating explosion that has been needed.

I am astounded, leveled and relaxed.

My temple a sphere of pure nothingness.

You have taken me here.

I think back repeatedly, ponder over this scene for days and sometimes even after the next or even

Three more have occurred.

It's just that, when it comes to you, I want you so bad, so often, that I am never fully satiated, even

AFTER the best climax heard in history.

So even in a setting where I cannot get to you, you are sitting in my head, naked, nervous and always

Ready to start something.

## *Devilish*

I wanna pin you,

Up against the fridge,

Make you succumb to me,

Eat my pussy,

Slop it up with your tongue,

Slip your hand inside,

Do what I fucking tell you.

Now

FUCK

Harder,

Until I say stop

Let me tie you up

You can't touch me anymore

I will lick you

Tickle you,

Tease the fuck out of you.

Bite you begging,

Screaming for more.


And I laugh, I will


Fuck you later, when I want it again.

## *Sometimes all I think about all day is your pussy.*

But it never starts there

How my hands slide over your skin

So soft, So beautiful, So amazing.

I am imagining running my fingers all over you.

The delicate balance of pushing into you

Kneading your skin, and pulling my hands down.

Kissing as I go too.

I love to kiss your neck,

Hear you giggle as I move down.

Move onto your back, and nibble my way along there.

Reaching around to feel how erect your nipples are.

Know how turned on you are

And now I know when I get to where I really want to go

How wet you will be.

The anticipation of this is hard to resist

And sometimes I can't

Sometimes I must go directly there,

To where my mind rests all day.

To where I am kept captive by my imagination

Where you keep me because you know I never want to leave

I have to go there

Sometimes that urge is just too strong.

All I want is to caress you, to hear you and to know you're satisfied.

I do need to feel you though

To feel how wet you get

How much you want me

Because that is how much I want you.

I sometimes need to rush in these instances

But mostly I like to take my time

Travel the course of your body

Explore how every part of you feels.

Every slip, sliding piece of flesh I can get my hands and fingers over.

How damn good it feels

I use your sweet noises,

Your coos

And your smile to guide me

I stroke along your thigh

Teasing and moving up,

Getting equally as flustered in the wait

In denying myself the pleasure of what I want

I am denying you the pleasure you know you will get

But that is half the fun.

I enjoy the manipulations of your body

Doing what I can to make you get as wet as I know you can get

And I tease a bit

I like to push and to pull

And to temper how I enter

But once I do, I can't hold back

On my mind is one thing,

The one final thing,

All I can think of is the noises you make as you come

The gush that happens when you do

How it drips down my arm

Slides down and makes me so wet I can almost come

I said almost

But I don't want to stop

Its all about you now

But it is a little about me too

My ego

How I feel knowing I have made you come

God its good

That rush

To know I have made you feel great, amazing, magnificent.

To know I have changed your day

Started it right

Ended it right

Made it a good lunch break

The kind you never want to end

Call in sick after lunch

But no one is fooled

They all know why

Just knowing I have made you come

Not just once but twice

Oh wait make that three times.

Mm that's good.

The best part of my day then is later

When I can still smell you on my finger tips

Though I thought I washed my hands well enough

I guess I didn't but ok.

But that's ok.

It makes me wonder..

Hmmm... if I dare to lick them

Could I still taste you?

This thought brings visions of your face as you come

And the post coitus flush you exude

And this excites me yet again

Wow

I can hardly wait to get home.

## *Blow pony*

I push you up against the wall,

Dancing hasn't been enough.

Kissing here is run by the movement of the crowd.

I need more.

More control, more force

I want to show you how bad I need you

Then, there

Literally climbing beams so that I can be part of you

So, into the moment I don't care about being stripped on the floor.

No one exists.

It is just us.

Or does the crowd make it more.

Is it part of seducing the audience?

The part that I love so much

Or is it you and how much I imagine being inside of you.

How creamy and wet you must be

The smooth skin I know

And the delicious parts I haven't been allowed to touch yet.

The beat of the music just adds to the frenzy.

Pushing, pulling, begging for more

But knowing we shouldn't

You sneak your hands up my shirt

The trepidation mixed with desire is evident as I moan with anticipation

So fast, so firm but patient,

Inch by inch

I push your hand up

My impatience wins.

You smile and continue our tryst.

My hands shimmy to your ass

Pulling you closer

This gives enough privacy for a little more action

Below the clothes we dip.

Until we've pulled them down too far

Yes, you are dripping.

I couldn't help myself.

My hand snaps back as you begrudgingly pull it out.

You're not quite the exhibitionist I am.

Your face clouds with mild embarrassment,

I look on,

Finally seeing the scores of people around us

They have given us a wide berth

Were they watching us

Or are they as oblivious as we were to them?

I turn, smile and I ask, 'time to go home?"

Yes.

## *I want to unwrap you like the present you are*

An excited child at Christmas

Wondering what the ribbons hide

What the paper is keeping from me

Below the surface

Antsy as soon as I see the box

From the moment I meet you

Never able to fully anticipate what I might find

Wiggling, jittery with curiosity, longing

Always knowing it is the best thing I could ever possibly want

Untangling the bow

Part of what you hold the surface

Pull off the first corner

Just a bit from your high school years

Finding the folds that come out of it

Your history, growing up, learning to drive

Every rip something new

Every pull another admission

Do I dare

Want to?
I unwarp you like a child that has stared at the these presents for ages

full of excitement

Wonderment

And fulfillment at finally getting to see

What is hidden on the inside

I' am waiting for you to come to me

And it may take months

Holidays and presents are always worth their wait

Will you let me unwrap you like I want to?

Let me lovingly unwrap that carefully constructed

Brilliantly bright box

(the piece I 'm so excited to unwrap?)

I know it holds your heart

Can I have your heart

Will you gift me your heart in a box?

Give me the chance to know it fully

This is what excites me when we first start talking.

## *Cunt jumping*

Every situation has its own rituals

These two were no different.

We drive, we pay

We are literally signing our lives away.

We murmur and we prepare

but really are we prepared?

The exchange on the dance floor,

Closeness, light touches as you pass.

Heated looks, electric.

Licking my lips a little more,

Talking a little quieter,

Leaning in a little closer,

Smelling a little sweeter.

Our suits are ridiculous,

Laughing as we shimmy into them

Anxiety escaping our lips

Trying not to recognize

The monumental thing

We are about to do.

Suddenly we're intertwined

Our bodies moving together

Hands exploring,

Every touch I awaken

A tingle in a new place

So lost I didn't realize how wet I'd become.

Every finger tip a drop

Rippling out


Each time;

Walking to the plane,

Into your house,

It all starts with the nervousness,

The hesitancy about what may go wrong.


I signed up for this

These adventures

Both dangerous

Exhilarating

Exiting

Pushing past my boundaries

And this time

I decide I'm going in first.

You take my fist like its nothing,

I am wrapped inside you

I can feel the beat,

The bump,

The edges

Your skin enticing me to push further

To go deeper

It's a game we are playing

Give and take

And I am on board

The plane, its old, it is rickety,

They say it is safe

Like you're safe

I am strapped into the gear

I am ready for this,

I think

Rising I still have a chance to say no.

But it's do or die time

And I've been handed over for consumption.


Your lips are seeking my mouth,

Reaching, probing

Asking for more,

Seeking more,

Tiptoeing down my neck

Tracing lines around my nipples,

Hands steady on my hips

Fingering the line of my boxers,

Playfully, purposely.

Sitting on the bench I scoot,

Slowly, steadily,

Each inch forward,

Each inch in

I am more committed to the action,

As I dangle on the edge

I am asked one more time,

Are you sure?

You coax me,

Purring praises in my ear

        You're so wet,

        You feel so good

        We're almost there.

And I respond,

Body a little slicker,

Succulent, sliding

I ask for more.


Teetering on the edge

I know I am about to face

Everything I ever knew

Here, now in this moment,

This empty blue sky.

Ready?

Again, I nod.

Here we go.


I am to the point of aching for you.

I push.

More please I ask.

Baby they're all there.

You tell me I am definitely ready.

You begin to tease a little more,

Tracing the outline of my slit,

Baby, I don't know how much


Inhale, exhale


Much more I can take,

I...

Leap.

The air surrounds me,

Lifting.

I've control

Only things I can do is surrender.

Trust the instructor,

They have the controls.

Every fiber in my body is here,

Is now,

Nothing exists.

You're pushing inside me

As fast and as hard as you can,

My juices stream down your arm

You follow it up to my lips,

A quick lick

My body is ready,

And you can feel it,

I know it and I spread myself,

I am flying,

Drifting

Soaring,

In patterns

And lust.

Though clouds above the world,

Laughing

Nothing defines me at this point.


But time stops as my body suck you in,

My cunt surrounding your fist,

Clenching

Trying to nestle in deeper

I gasp

And erupt

The pleasure

So intense its almost excruciating.

Filling and releasing

Collapsing and expanding

I am everything and I am nothing.


I am pushed to the limit of my body

And the pleasure explodes

Nothing exists but it and you

Even the holder of the hand,

 The controller of the parachute

Neither matters in this moment

My body has been given over to the exquisite

And my life has never been the same.


Jumping out of a plane

Getting fisted for the first time

Both the most memorable experiences

 Of this person's life.

Comparable, yeah

The same, not really

Life changing, ab-so-fucking-lutely.

## *Cum stains*

I love cum stains

The ones left on the bed.

I wait to wash the sheets

Revel in our desire

Sleeping in our love

Our sweetness,

Our ecstasy.

And I take pictures

Hang them on the wall like Rorschach blots.

They're magnificent.

        Round edges,

        Sharp edges,

        Vague shapes,

        Sometimes a descriptive picture

        And other times just drops in a line

        Dribbling from my pussy as I lay there

        Exhaling deeply.

The messy love smells,

        Gushy deliciousness,

                Tastes so sweet,

                      Looks so

divine

It is art,

Magical lustful art.

    People comment "how beautiful"

            "oh I took those"

    "such talent, they're great."

And I tell them,           cum stains.

    They begin to blush

    A brilliant chartreuse,

            "what" I smirk.

These,

These are badges of honor.

To make someone cum

Sometimes so hard they project,

Expanding beyond their body,

Allowing their essence our,

Sticky sweet flavorful juices

 For me to taste,

To savor,

To devour

Nothing is more heavenly,

I promise.

            I'm proud.

As they scan the scenery

They darken,

Almost maroon.

But I can see the twinkle in their eye

as they look at my camera.

## *Fruity*

I am sitting here

Cutting fruit for the dinner I am preparing

One full of summer and sweetness and discovery

One with you in mind

A ripe succulent pear

Perfect in contour

And texture

So Juicy, all I can think about is later

When I will be fucking you

How deliciously wet you get

How ready you are for me when I get to you

It doesn't help that you are texting me dirty things

Distracting things

Provocative, yummy things

Things for before dinner

Some for after

And maybe a bit for in-between

As I cut the overtly ripe fruit

I slowly put the pieces in my mouth

I lick at them, seductively placing them on my tongue

Pulling them in and licking my fingers

You are nowhere near me at the moment

But I know later I will describe to you what I having been doing

What I am thinking of as I suck on the ripe fruit

As it puddles in my mouth when I press

Similar to your lips, luscious, tantalizing and completely saturated

My body reacts to the moist sweet flavor

I tense with the desire creeping into every inch of me

The viscous flow of nerves that are on fire

Racing with electric blood to be touched

And when I hit the counter just the right way on accident

A wave of pleasure flows through me knowing I will be at your hands

Touching you, you touching me, getting to that secret spot

The one only you seem to have found

For now I am left to cut this seemingly now orgasmic fruit

I can't wait to eat you later... I mean uhh it...

## *Hot*

I want to get with you,

feel your hands sliding into those places

I keep to myself,

let the release of you out of me.

Stop being so closed in and let the lioness out,

I need.

I know you can make me

I know you feel it too.

Tell me you want me,

tell me you want to touch me,

now, tell me how, make it happen.

Make me succumb to you,

let me take every breath away as you slip slide

and feel me, arouse me, define me

How do you like it?

Pull my hair, bite my lips,

lick every inch of me that I never see,

spread me, take me to that space,

that place, the one in my head,

where I slide into when you are fist deep inside.

When I feel the gush,

that tingling release of every inch of me that I hold so tightly

but you make me come so quickly.


Will you just fuck me?

Put your hands on me?

Kiss me, hit me, and bite me

Suck me and bruise me

I want you so deep inside me I can't breathe

Have you in that spot

Where I shudder and shake with every movement

With every time you rock

With every contraction

And every moan.

I want your hands wrapped around my throat,

My wrists, and my thighs

Restraint and Push

Pull and ache

Fight

You know what I want

I don't want to ask

I want you to take it

I know you want me to beg for it though

And I like to oblige you.


You requested me tonight

But I am more eager to have you.

Because when I take you and you come

It is magic

It leaves me ready and waiting

The setting in my cunt is on high

In fact as I hear you

As I feel you

I am so very close anyway

All you have to do now is touch me.

## *I don't think you understand how nervous you make me*

I don't think you understand how nervous you make me and in seeing that it makes me even more nervous. Am I avoiding because of that? I don't want to. But I know the creepy clingy type… happens to me a lot and I refuse to be one of those. So I suppress the urge and then possibly seem more distant. Maybe if I give you up again you will crawl back around. Maybe if I deny you, you will want more. Maybe if I stop obsessing (see this rant/rave), it will happen. But damn it. Everything is so new and it always is everytime but this has not happened to me in a long time and I am no good at dealing, so I obsess, think, analyze to an extreme. Question everything, myself included. Is this real? Am I sure? What may happen? What is the worst? Possible hopes, dreams, aspirations, everything. I just need a message to tell me I am not barking up the wrong tree, not imagining things, seeing what I think I see and not hoping when I see there is no hope. I want, I want, I want, seems to be my recurring theme. I have no idea if you are a good kisser or what your bedroom style is. I have no clue what you like or what you want but thoughts of me raking my finger nails across your back turn me on, thoughts of holding on as tight as I can, thoughts of squeezing, pulling, digging, making you jump with the feeling, cry out a little "ow." But all the while know you like it. Giggling at your pain, asking you to run your hands through my hair and pull. No, harder.

Do what you do. Let me figure you out. I can be as vocal as you want.

God, I want to find out.

## *We met after long conversations, took a walk, someplace nice.*

We met after long conversations, took a walk, someplace nice. So sweetly, slowly, and lingering we stride. You touch me to make a point. I revel in that touch. Your smell wafts towards me; so Beautiful, a sweet, flowery fragrance. I want to kiss you, so bad, so much. We walk into a grove of trees. Secluded, yet open. You push me against a tree and kiss me, hard. I reach for you. Put my hands on your neck and pull you closer. I slide up to your hair, grab a bit and pull. You let out a longing sigh. I pull a little harder, not much though; I don't want to hurt you. I kiss your neck, slide my hands down your arms, to your hips and pull you into me so we bump a little, a hint of adventures to come. You start kissing my neck, slide a hand to my breast, oh my, that feels good. You reach down to pull off my shirt, as you come back up and take my exposed nipple in your mouth. I am wet as an overly ripe orange waiting to be picked and I will be, soon. I reach to your pussy; it is warm and inviting. I rub just a little as you moan. I reach up and pull your head back down to my nipple. I reach back towards your pussy, this time undo your pants, and reach inside. Mmm so warm, so wet, I slip my finger inside your lips. I feel your clit, I sweep over it, continue to run my fingers over your beautiful lips. I pull my hand out and slip my own fingers into my mouth, tasting you. You look up and you smile.

## *I want to hear it*

All of it

Every last thing you have

I want to hear you scream

I want to fall into the gutteral noises you make as you come

I want to catch the air escaping your lungs as you release

I want to listen to the involuntary noises you make as I touch you

I want to hear the pleasure I have given

I want to pick up on every inch I have climbed

Every bit of skin I have caressed

Everything I have done

I want to take in every kiss I have given

Every bite you have received

Every time my tongue touched your skin

I want to hear it

I want to devour the Oh oh oh

I want to hear every time I have crawled into you

And every time I have withdrawn

Only to have you beg to continue

I want to hear it

Every time your nipples get hard as I surround them with my mouth

Every time I have rubbed you just right

Sucked you right

Pulled you right

Moved you just right

Every time I have touched something in that pleasant tease

The "fuck" out of you way that I do it

Round about

Not quite touching

Lightly running my tongue

My fingers over

Then attacking

Hard, fast, and steady

I want to hear you come

I want to follow every time I have made you smile

Every time you thought about me and got turned on

Every time you have every masturbated to the thought of me

Every time you say me and immediately got wet because of all of this

I want to hear it

I want to listen to how your body quakes when we are done

How you can't stand

Your legs are weak

Your whole body is weak

How you need to take a moment

Or a few minutes

Before you are able to function again

I like the little end moments

The cuddling

Simply breathing

Just enjoying

Taking in all that has happened

Pure in the moment action

I want to hear it

The gush of your juices

The readiness of your hips

Lips and hands

The eager anticipation of your lips

The noisy smack as I hit your ass

The sigh as I pull hair

The giggle when I tug just right

**Sigh** I love that giggle

I want to monitor the climb as you ride

The quickening of your breath

The small sounds, as you get hotter

Wetter

Closer

MMM there it goes

# Cunt Jumping 2
# An Ode to the Orgy

awkward

standing there

no one knows what to expect

but we all know why we came

to come

glancing around

everyone take inventory

who do they want to touch

what do they want to touch

even with clothes on, we all know what lies beneath

wet puddles of delicious

body parts to pinch

bite

lick

suck

suddenly our imaginations are on fire

embers burning in our eyes

a collective sign

whispering

furtive giggles

preemptive cuddling

lightly stroking skin

a kiss here

hesitation


as we begin to push forward

each party seeking

moving a little farther down

hands on thighs

asses embraced

breasts

gently and tenderly

defiantly caressed

we all have consented to this

but you hear often

"is this okay?"

"do you like that?

or the most important question

with the usual answer of I don't know

"what do you want?"


with each fingertip

we move forward

carefully and successfully

within a few hours

all so wrapped

into each others bodies

roaming landscape of consumption

hands in places previously denied

moans of pain

of pleasure

                                                                              escaping

moving through the room

through the crowd

we are all starting to echo off of each other

one person growls

giving the whole room a new round of pleasure

pure energy

exquisite

flowing out of us

into us

the room smelling not so discreetly of sex

tasty


audible sounds

coming from every side

skin hitting skin

sometimes rhythmic

other times sudden

sweet exhale

a grunt of increased satisfaction

reverberating

leading to harder

longer

gasps

precious murmers

yes,

please,

more

gifts of noise

desire

pleasure spelled out

release

dancing across the air

intertwined in each other

floating over

into and through

humming

cascading down

hitting our thighs

our stomachs

rolling off of us easily

slick and supple

dripping

soft skin

providing the balance

tasting of sweetness

and sweat

of wonder

and creation

tactile

electric

throbbing

every beat grabbing

wrapping fingers

up and in

legs gripping

body parts

aching

grasping

a constant wave

undulating

push and pull

gritty

changing

rearranging

bodies never completely apart

rolling over

into

so entrapped

no distinct end

draping limps

soft glow of ecstasy

intoxicating

invigorating

subtle glances

changes

movements

creating a new scene

forever lifting

sweet kisses

sometimes hard

bumping

gyrating


everything in play

scenary switched

within seconds

for hours

time lapse

revolving

repeating

moving again

something new

this dance is delicately drawn

but masterfully crafted


it starts with a little tap

## Wolfs warning

I am the wolf

On the prowl

Ready for something new

Dressed in such a way

You are fooled

Delicious to look at

Daring you to take a bite

Coy and teasing

You'll never get enough

I won't let you

I am the wolf

You can't trap the wolf

I will dig under your skin

Get into your head

Creep around your thoughts

Until I have taken over

I am the wolf

Sheep beware

I will get you,

Make you nervous

You won't notice when I get in

Never knew you were fooled

The con is good

 You can't actually see it

I am the wolf

Sharp teeth

Piercing eyes

My laugh may not be menacing

But I am

 As I get close to you

Brilliantly smiling

Smelling sweet

Loving you in that way

You never knew

 You wanted so bad

I have warned you

See me for what I am

I am the wolf

An excellent loner

 Not meant to be held down

Taking everything, I want

Only giving back when I decide

Choosing where I go

What things I do

Never truly wanting to be alone

 I am the wolf

Entering your garden

Stealing daisy's

Your heart

Dangerous all the same

I've told you approach with caution

Be wary

Handle me carefully

Unless you are prepared to lie with the wolf

It could be the best adventure you've ever had.

## *Holding onto both sides of the coin*

Wrapping my hands around it

Feeling the curves

Your curves

The edges

The hard parts

Learning each side

Learning you

Knowing the ridges

The good ones

The jagged ones

The places where you are tender

And the hardened ones that no one gets to

The falls

The bumps

The nicks

Every piece of your body

 I've successfully mapped

Created the proper algorithm in my head

The ones that get you to the whole places faster

Flipping you over again like this coin in my hand

Learning each side

 Knowing every texture

Having memorized the thing

So much it never leaves my fingers knowledge

Even when a phantom in my hand

I still know

I flip this coin repeatedly in my hand

I'm thinking of you

Of what you are to me

Suddenly you've become the coin

the thing I hold onto so deeply feeling both sides

Wrapping my hands around you.

## *Techniques*

You have to excite her, coach her, parley with her

Pump her

Push her

And prepare her

Three times before she's ripe, set and waiting

Sometimes less

Sometimes more

But three is usually the magic number

Enough to get everything wet and sticky and slick

Eager for action

Once you have figured out the exact number

All you need to do now is make the last part of the connection

The sweet wonderful connection

The first time will be the hardest

But you need to make her sing

After this first time, she is easy

It no longer takes much to keep her flowing

It takes some skill, some gift and some charm

Most people think its basic

And that it may come naturally

Which is does

Kind of

But you are still required to have a certain amount of cunning and clout

You must learn how to make her purr

Make her climb like you crave

The push and the pull

The slow steady pace

The tango you dance with her

Roll her

Manipulate her

And make her proceed as you command

You advance her

Make her toe the line without going over

What you do is an art

Beauty follows you as you advance

As you frolic, strut, twist, sway, swirl, and then electrify

Every corner you traverse is stunning

The precision and the deliberation

Amazing

You are directionally talented and focused

All things that aid in your quest

You conduct her

And now you are learning to tend certain domains

These areas require you to be attentive and patient

To handle with care like a choice blossom

Manage discreetly

Yet with full intent and desire

Take your time

Make sure you have covered every inch

Carefully

Pushing the edges,

Gliding her through

Feeling every detail

Savor them like you relish your own form

Now make sure you allow for a second inspection

It is always recommended

The extra diligence pays off

Immensely in the long run

And the more copious you are

The more accessible she is

You are well versed in your actions

You know the curves

The mounts, the valleys

And the hills

Once you have all this grasped you can then start to deviate

The artistry is in the movement

So try a new direction

Change courses

Make your own adventure

Again you are an artist and you are magnificent

Picasso, Monet, Pollock

The comparisons are in monumental supply

You can do anything you set your mind to

And it will be greatly appreciated

The compliments will stream in

You will be revered

Coveted and sought after

Guidelines and shared knowledge

But some secrets you should always keep to yourself

Everyone loves the person who has mastered a craft

And you my friend have that proficiency

Now can I please have my lawn mower back?

www.ingramcontent.com/pod-product-compliance
Lightning Source LLC
Chambersburg PA
CBHW030116100526
44591CB00009B/419